Special Thanks:
Thank you to those who bought my 1st book. It gave me the courage to continue and share more of myself through these books. I hope all who read this book as well as my other books are inspired to dream BIG and act on them.

I want to be my best self.
There are BIG dreams inside of me.

But where can I start,
so others can share the
dreams I see.

Maybe we can ask for help?
I know what we can do!
Let's ask Mr. Goodwin. He
can help us.

Even you!

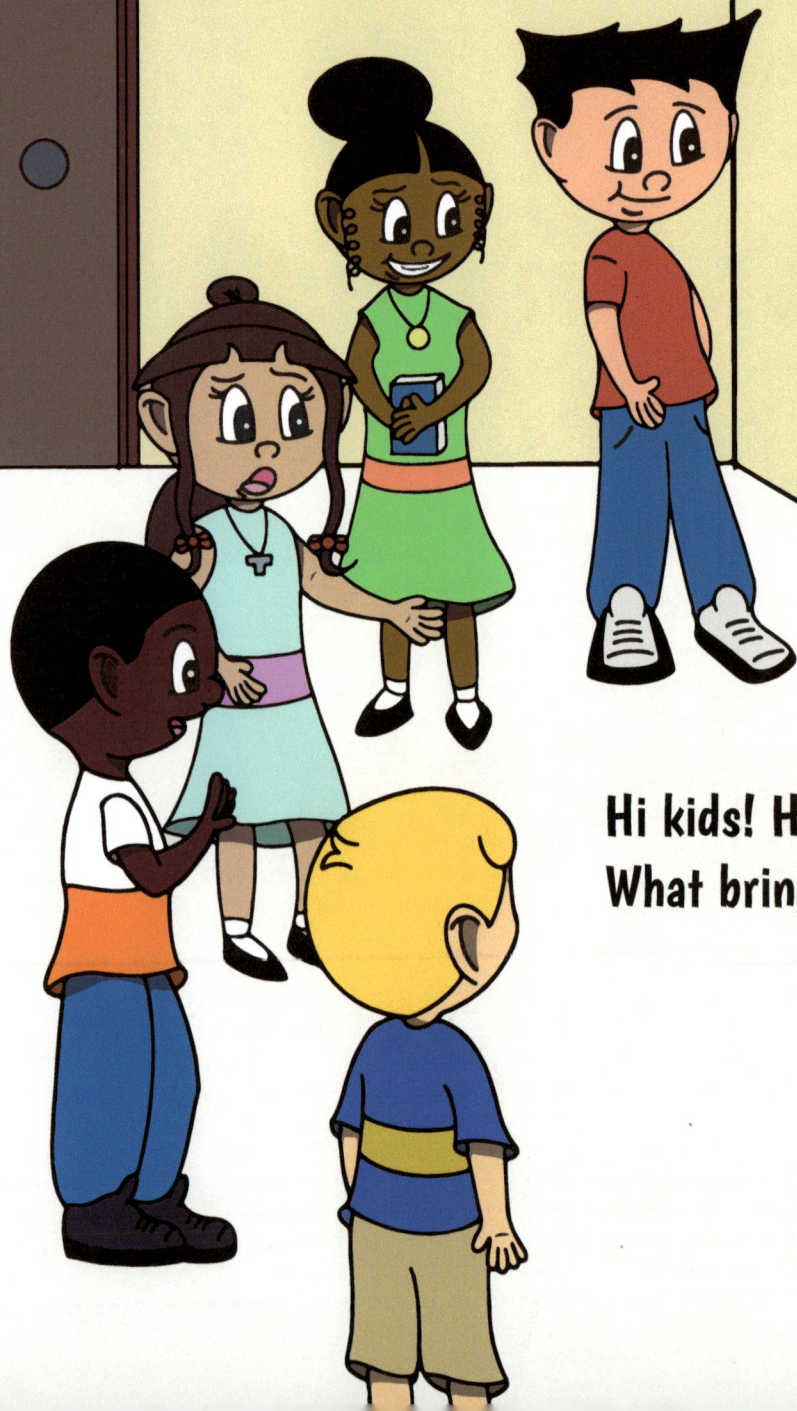

Hi kids! How are you?
What brings you in?

We all have big dreams, but
don't know the steps to begin.

Well listen up everyone.
Would you all like to learn?

I'll share with you each step, and help you become DREAM BUILDERS.

So what are your dreams?
Would you like to share?

We'll all help each other along.
I'll give you the tools to prepare.

Alright young Dream Builders.
Let's get started right away.
Before we begin building,
let's go over the steps first.
Okay?

Step 1 to building your dreams
is the easiest and most fun.
Think about your
dreams, using
your...

Step 2 are your WORDS!
Share your dreams with
smiles on your face.

It's ok if others don't understand your dreams at first.
Just stay focused on YOUR race.

Imagination

The more you imagine
and the more you speak,

WORDS

you'll start to do the things
you both say and think.

Step 3 is ACTION.
You're all doing so great.
Are you excited? Your
dreams are beginning to
take shape.

Acting on your dreams may not be easy.
What you're doing is all so new.

Keep moving forward anyways.
After all, your dreams are waiting
for you to build it too.

Color Wheel

Step 4 are **HABITS.** You're working daily on your dreams.

A R T

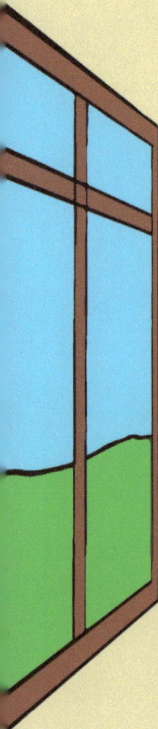

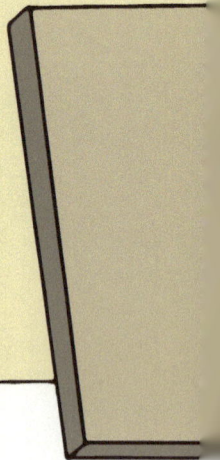

Well done young Dream Builder.
What a sight your dreams have
come to be.

Step 5 is CHARACTER.
Wow! You all have come
so far.

I'm so proud of all of you.
Your dreams have become
who you are.

These are the steps my friends,
to build any dream of any size.
Building your dreams is the greatest
adventure. The journey is an amazing ride.

So, if there's a dream inside of you
wanting to be set free.

Build it no matter how hard because,
out of your challenge will come your
victory.

DREAM

BIG

About the Author:

Thank you for coming along with me on this adventure. I've spent years reading about leadership and growing myself. After working with students for many years, I thought about being able to share leadership principles in a story format during a child's foundational years. It's my belief that when someone decides to build their dreams, what's most important in the beginning is building their foundation first. It's our foundations that our dreams are built and stand on. It's my hope that my books will be an effective tool and assist in laying down the foundation for people to grow and build their dreams. Thank you!

www.ingramcontent.com/pod-product-compliance
Lightning Source LLC
Chambersburg PA
CBHW042006100426
42736CB00038B/85